# The Goalie from Nowhere

**Alan MacDonald**

Illustrated by Jane Cope

# 1

# The cup final

*And there it is, the final whistle. Ditchley Rovers have won! Their first Wembley cup final in history! The players are dancing around and hugging each other. The crowd (three parents and a kid in a pushchair) is going wild.*

*Joss Porter, Ditchley's three-goal hero, is carried shoulder high by his team mates. He raises the cup to the crowd… these are amazing scenes!*

I'm Joss Porter, in case you hadn't guessed.

I do commentaries like that in my head all the time. At school, on the bus, even underwater in the bath.

But this commentary was different. It wasn't a dream. Ditchley Rovers really *were* about to play in our first Wembley final on Saturday.

Okay, it wasn't at Wembley Stadium. It was at Wembley Park. And okay, the pitch at Wembley Park has hardly any grass and dips in the middle like a banana. But that didn't matter to me. We were in the cup final and I was perfecting my commentary for Saturday.

Of course, it wouldn't turn out like that in real life. We couldn't actually win. We were playing Valley Kings in the final.

They'd won the cup three times in a row. Deep down, I knew we didn't stand a chance against them. We'd be lucky to score a single goal. But then you never knew what might happen in football.

Who would have expected Baggy
Shorts to turn up out of nowhere?

# 2

# Baggy Shorts

It was Thursday evening, two days before the cup final. We'd all met up for a practice session over at Wembley Park.

Dad called us together for a team talk. As usual, he was wearing his navy tracksuit with the England 1966 badge on the pocket.

'Now we all know that Saturday is a big game for us,' he said. 'Our Joss has been going to bed with his kit on every night. Just to make sure he doesn't miss the kick-off.'

Everyone looked at me and laughed. I hated it when Dad made stupid jokes about me. Sometimes I wished he wasn't our manager.

Dad went on. 'A cup final is special. There are plenty of kids who'd like to be in your boots on Saturday. But they're not. It's your chance, so make the most of it.'

I looked around. Matt, Flip, Sammy, Nasser and the rest were nodding their heads. You could see they were as keen as I was.

We lined up for shooting practice against Flip, our goalie.

'Ouch! Joss! Why don't you break my fingers or something?' he said as he stopped one of my thunderbolts.

The truth is, Flip's a good goalie. If it wasn't for him, we'd never have reached the cup final. In the semi-final he'd made a string of blinding saves.

We were dead lucky in that game. Everything went right for us. I'd even scored a late winner with my knee.

Dad said that if we'd been playing Man United, the goalposts would have crashed down and injured half their team during the warm-up.

Flip's not very big for a goalie but he's quick and brave. He has to be because our attack is a lot better than our defence.

This evening Flip was in great form. He'd dive to stop a shot and spring up again like a jack-in-the-box. Hardly anything got past him.

A cold wind blows across Wembley Park on a winter evening. A thin mist drifted over from the river.

It was Nasser who noticed a strange-looking kid watching us from behind the goal.

'Hey, Joss,' he grinned. 'You seen old Baggy Shorts over there? Think he wants a game?'

I looked behind the goal. The kid was standing to one side of the posts with a ball tucked under his arm.

He was tall and skinny like a runner bean. His huge shorts came down to his knees and flapped in the wind. Above a green roll-neck jumper, his big ears stuck out like mug handles. And on top, he wore a flat grey cap. He looked like a jumble sale on legs.

By now Sammy, Matt, and the others had seen him. They started sniggering.

'D'you see that kit, eh?'

'Is that Arsenal's away strip?'

'No, it must be Oxfam's.'

'Let's sign him up. He can be our secret weapon.'

'Yeah! He can hide the match ball in his shorts.'

Nasser said the last joke too loud because Baggy Shorts frowned and looked at the ground.

'Shut up!' I hissed. 'He'll hear you.'

A few minutes later, I went to get a ball from behind the goal. Baggy Shorts was still standing there. The cold didn't seem to bother him. I wondered why he kept watching us.

'Hello,' I said. 'You from round here?'

He touched his cap and nodded seriously. 'Used to be.'

'What happened? Did you move away?'

'Kind of.'

There was a pause. 'I'm a goalie,' he said, looking straight at me.

'Are you?' I said.

'Yes. I'm a good goalie.'

'I bet you are. But we've already got a goalie. He's over there.'

I jerked my thumb towards Flip. Baggy Shorts nodded again.

'I'm a good goalie,' he repeated, bouncing his own ball and catching it in his big pale hands. It was a funny kind of football, made of heavy brown leather and held together by a yellow lace.

'We're playing here on Saturday in the cup final,' I said. 'Come and watch if you want.'

Baggy Shorts nodded again. 'I never played in a final. Never.' He looked away into the distance as if something was just out of sight. The mist had got thicker.

I said, 'Well, kick-off's at three. Come and support us.' I realized I was shivering. 'I've got to go now...'

At that moment I heard a loud yell of pain. I ran back to the others. The shooting practice had stopped.

Everyone was standing round Flip. He was sitting on the ground. Dad was kneeling beside him, looking at his nose which was an ugly swollen red.

'Ah! Don't touch it!' he cried out.

'What happened?' I asked.

'I didn't know he was coming for the cross,' said Sammy. 'I was jumping to head the ball and Flip came out. Somehow… I headed him instead.'

'It was *my* ball,' moaned Flip. 'I called for it.'

'Will he be all right?' I asked Dad. 'For Saturday, I mean? He will be able to play on Saturday, won't he?'

Dad helped Flip to his feet. 'It's probably just a nasty bruise. But I'll take him to the hospital to get it looked at. Just in case. The rest of you better go home. It's getting late.'

We trooped off the field miserably.

'Nice one, Sammy,' I said. 'If Flip can't play on Saturday, there goes our only chance. Without him, Valley Kings will murder us.'

As we were leaving I remembered Baggy Shorts again. I turned back to wave goodbye. But he'd gone, melted away into the fog.

# 3

# The goalie always gets the blame

We were sitting in the dressing room in silence, all staring at the floor. Dad had just asked if anyone wanted to play in goal.

The news about Flip was bad. The hospital said his nose was broken. There was no way he could play in a cup final.

We had to play our substitute, Gormless Gordon. Dad put him at right back. That was where he would do least damage.

We took the news about Flip as if someone had died.

There was no point in kidding ourselves any longer. We'd lost the cup final before the game started.

I could hear the commentary
running through my head:

*And it's another one! This time
through the goalkeeper's legs. This
is turning into a massacre. 32-0
to Valley Kings and there's still
half an hour to go! Ditchley
Rovers must wish the final
whistle would blow and put
them out of their misery.*

That's why no one wanted to put on
the green jersey. The goalie always gets
the blame. He's the one the rest of the
team pick on when they're getting
hammered. That's why I couldn't
believe it when Dad spoke to me.

'Joss, you've played in goal before.'

I looked up in horror. 'That was only
messing around in the park. I've never
played in a proper match.'

'There's always a first time. You could do it.'

'Dad! No way! I'm a striker. I'd be hopeless in goal.'

'Well, somebody's got to. Listen all of you. Flip isn't coming. We've just got to put out the best team we can. And if we lose it's no disgrace. Now I'll ask again – is anyone willing to go in goal?'

I looked around at the rest of the team. Begging them: *Not me! Anyone but me. Somebody else do it, please!*

No one would look at me. They
stared at the floor as if they wanted to
crawl underneath it.

'Right. That's it then. Joss, you're in
goal first half,' said Dad. He was getting
angry.

I picked up the green jersey he threw
at me. It wasn't fair. He shouldn't be
manager if he was going to pick on me.

Valley Kings were already out on the pitch in their smart new strip. Red and white striped shirts with their names on the back. Just like professionals.

'Come on you Kings! You'll murder this lot!' shouted their manager from the touch line. Most of their team were bigger than us.

I recognized Gary Spencer. He's top scorer for our school team. He gave me a nod.

'Hi, Joss! They're not playing you in goal are they?'

I nodded miserably.

'You *must* be desperate,' he said rubbing his hands together. You could see him counting all the goals he was going to score.

The game kicked off. Valley Kings
sent the ball straight down the wing.
We didn't clear it. A high ball came
over. I started to come out for it. Then I
changed my mind.

As I tried to get back, the ball
thumped into the corner of the net.
Gary Spencer turned away with his arms
going like windmills.

'Goooooooooal!'

Nasser shook his head at me in disbelief. 'Why didn't you come out?'

'Why didn't you mark him if you're so great?' I snapped back.

The rest of the first half we defended grimly, hardly ever getting past the half-way line. Valley Kings went two up after twenty minutes.

After that, I made a few lucky saves. And we kept the score down by keeping ten players back and booting the ball anywhere.

As the minutes ticked toward half-time, I noticed the mist drifting in again from the river. I heard a ball bounce behind me.

And there was Baggy Shorts.

He was wearing the same kit as before. Grey cap, green jumper, huge, baggy white shorts.

'Hi,' I said. 'Come to watch us get beaten?'

He stood to one side of my goal.

'Where's your goalie?' he asked.

'Broke his nose. Couldn't come.
That's why they stuck me in goal.'

He nodded thoughtfully. 'I'm a
goalie,' he said.

'Yes. You told me that the other day.'
'I'm good.'
'But you don't play for our team.'
'I could do, though.'

Baggy Shorts took off his flat cap and held it in both hands. His hair was cut short over his big ears and parted in the middle.

He looked at me, his eyes full of longing.

'Please. I never played in a final. Never. Give me a chance.'

It came out in a rush. Then he put his cap back on and waited.

At that moment, the referee blew for half-time.

# 4

# Everyone deserves their chance

'You must be bonkers, Joss,' said Sammy.
'Look at him. He turns up out of
nowhere in his grandma's bloomers and
you want to play him in goal.'

'But we haven't got a goalie,' I
argued. 'We're going to get beaten
anyway. What have we got to lose?'

'Another ten goals,' said Nasser.

I pulled off the green jersey.

'Well, who's going in goal for the second half then? I've done my bit.'

Nobody took the jersey from me. We all looked at Dad. It was up to him.

He stared across at Baggy Shorts who stood a little way off, bouncing his old leather ball.

'Everyone deserves their chance,' said Dad.

Gormless Gordon came off to let Baggy Shorts on as sub. I could see the Valley Kings team grinning as Baggy Shorts took the field.

He ran past them, shorts flapping in the wind and cap pulled down over his eyes.

Gary Spencer came up to me as we lined up for kick-off.

'Where'd you get him from then? On special offer at Tesco's?' he grinned.

I stared back at him coldly. I'd had enough of being the joke team. We were going to lose. But at least we could make a fight of it.

From the kick-off, Sammy passed to me. I burst through the middle. Valley Kings weren't ready for an attack and my pass found Nasser in the penalty area.

He shot first time, low into the corner. Goal! 2-1.

It was the start we needed to get back in the game. But it also stung Valley Kings awake.

They soon had the ball back up our end and Gary Spencer carved his way through our defence. He left three players on the ground as he raced into the penalty area.

There was only Baggy Shorts left between him and the goal.

Spencer looked up to pick his spot. It was too easy. But in that second, Baggy Shorts came racing off his line like a greyhound.

Spencer couldn't take it in. One minute he had the ball. The next, Baggy Shorts had whipped it off his boot and kicked it upfield.

The small crowd watching clapped.
Ditchley Rovers looked at each other in
amazement. Baggy Shorts wasn't just
good. He was brilliant.

For the rest of the game, Valley Kings
tried to find a way to beat our new
goalkeeper.

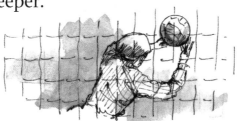

They aimed for the corners. They
rained in shots like cannonballs. They
tried to dribble round him.

But Baggy Shorts was a mind-reader.
He seemed to know exactly where the
ball was going.

He leapt like a cat and pulled it out of the air. He rolled over, sprang to his feet, bounced the ball twice and sent it into orbit.

With just ten minutes to go, we got a goal back to level the scores at 2-2. Then, as the minutes ticked away, the disaster happened.

Gary Spencer went through again. And again, Baggy Shorts dived at his feet.

But this time, Spencer was waiting for it. He went sprawling over the goalie. He lay in the mud holding his leg.

'Ahh, ref! Penalty!'

Anyone could see he'd dived on purpose. Anyone except the ref. He blew his whistle and pointed to the penalty spot.

Spencer's leg was better in a flash. He decided to take the penalty himself. He winked at Baggy Shorts with a smug look on his face.

Baggy Shorts didn't argue with the ref. He didn't say a word. He just turned and went back to his goal-line.

I walked away to the half-way line feeling sick. Three minutes to go. And we were going to lose to the worst penalty ever given.

But as Spencer placed the ball I couldn't help myself. I always do the commentary for penalties in my mind.

*And the crowd are hushed. Baggy Shorts crouches on his line. Spencer takes a run-up. He hits it hard, low, into the corner…*

*It's… No! Baggy Shorts has saved it one-handed. An incredible save! Spencer has his head in his hands. Baggy Shorts gathers the ball. Sends a long kick upfield. Towards… ME! Help! Where is everybody?*

From our half I just kept running towards the other goal, waiting for someone to tackle me.

But nobody did. Their defence was as stunned as I was. And as their goalie came out I slipped the ball past him. It rolled gently over the line. Goal!

The whistle went soon after. Ditchley Rovers had won the cup. 3-2 with a dramatic late winner from deadly Joss Porter. Just as I'd said all along.

I was mobbed by the whole team. They jumped on top of me until we were all rolling around in the mud, laughing.

Dad was going round banging everybody on the back. I don't think he could quite believe it.

Then we had to line up to get the cup. Sammy said, 'Where's Baggy Shorts? He should go up first. He was man of the match.'

We looked around. But we couldn't find him. No one knew where he'd gone. I looked back to the goal mouth where he'd saved the penalty. There was no one there. Only a fine mist drifting in from the river.

# 5

# Player No.132

A few days after the cup final I was at home watching telly. Dad was at the table working on his cigarette card collection.

He's got boxes full of these old picture cards his uncle collected years ago. They showed famous footballers of the past with centre partings and toothy smiles.

I saw him stop with the glue in one hand and a card in the other. His face was pale. He was staring at something.

'What is it?' I asked.

Without a word, he handed me the card in his hand. On the back it said:

**Player number 132: Billy Mackworth.**
*Goalkeeper.*
Only 17, Mackworth was a brilliant goalkeeper for Spurs. In 1947 he should have become the youngest player to play at Wembley. Sadly he died in a car crash a few days before the game. He never played in a cup final.

There was no mistaking the picture. He looked older, but the two big ears still stuck out like mug handles under his grey cap. The eyes stared gravely into the distance.

It was Baggy Shorts.

# *About the author*

For as long as I can
remember I've always
enjoyed two things –
writing stories and
playing football! So *The
Goalie from Nowhere*
combines two of my
favourite interests.

   As a boy I loved to
look at my dad's collection of
cigarette cards. There were pictures of birds,
veteran cars, and, of course, famous
footballers. That's where the idea for Baggy
Shorts came from. I thought it would be
interesting to write a football story with a
mystery behind it.